WHO NEEDS MIDLIFE AT YOUR AGE?

WHO NEEDS MIDLIFE AT YOUR AGE?

A Survival Guide for Men Over 30

JACK ROBERTS, DICK GUNTHER & STAN GORTIKOV

 AVON
PUBLISHERS OF BARD, CAMELOT, DISCUS AND FLARE BOOKS

WHO NEEDS MIDLIFE AT YOUR AGE? A SURVIVAL GUIDE
FOR MEN OVER 30 is an original publication of Avon Books. This
work has never before appeared in book form.

Quotation by Martha Lear Copyright © 1973 by The New York
Times Company. Reprinted by permission.

AVON BOOKS
A division of
The Hearst Corporation
1790 Broadway
New York, New York 10019

Library of Congress Cataloging in Publication Data

Roberts, Jack.
   Who needs midlife at your age?

   1. Middle age—Anecdotes, facetiae, satire, etc.
2. Middle age—Quotations, maxims, etc. I. Gunther,
Dick. II. Gortikov, Stan. III. Title.
PN6231.M47R6 1983   808.88′2   83-90765
ISBN 0-380-84103-7

First Avon Printing, September, 1983

Dedicated to all the heroines of male midlife
(especially Dian, Lois and Barbara)

YOUR MIDLIFE ENTRANCE EXAM

Is the thought of your own mortality no longer unthinkable?

Have you noticed how much your old friends look like old friends?

Do you remember the taste of mom's cookies but forget where you ate lunch yesterday?

Do you recognize more names in the obituaries than in the box scores?

Is a trip out of town an inconvenience, not an opportunity?

Do you still care about the whales, but identify more with Jonah?

When she suggests a massage, do you take off your shoes?

Do all the other guys at the public urinals finish before you do?

Does the expiration date on the film box bring tears to your eyes?

Is the usual morning stiffness now located in your other joints?

Do the "authorities"—cop, doctor, bookie—all look like kids?

Are you forever calling the
family dog "Seymour"
(which is your son's name)?

Do you maintain a two-season wardrobe: fat and thin?

Are you more concerned about whether
you can than whether she will?

Do her hot flashes provide the newest warmth in your relationship?

Has scanning menus in
cafes become a squinting
challenge?

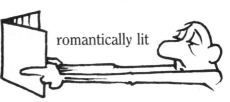

romantically lit

Do you greet the rise of your little friend
with gratitude rather than embarrassment?

Is your favorite sex position the one
which least hurts your back?

Did you finally give up the notion of becoming President
of the country, the company, or the Cub Scouts?

Did that exciting, fully packed bikini
turn out to be your daughter?

IF YOU ANSWERED YES TO MOST OF THESE QUESTIONS . . .

WELCOME.

Midlife begins with a gradual awareness that there's really a drop-off out there. This realization often coincides with another: young people behave as though they'll live forever . . . and you won't.

"The years between 50 and 70 are the hardest. You are always being asked to do things and you are not yet decrepit enough to turn them down." —T. S. ELIOT

"I don't believe one grows older. I think that what happens early on in life is that at a certain age one stands still and stagnates." —T. S. ELIOT

"Whoever, in middle age, attempts to realize the wishes and hopes of his early youth, invariably deceives himself. Each ten years of a man's life has its own fortunes, its own hazards, its own desires." —GOETHE

"We cannot live the afternoon of life according to the program of life's morning; for what was great in the morning will be little in the evening, and what in the morning was true will at evening have become a lie." —CARL JUNG

"Of all the barbarous middle ages, that which is most barbarous is the middle age of man; it is—I really scarce know what; but when we hover between fool and sage." —BYRON

"All things must change. To something new, to something strange." —LONGFELLOW

CRISIS.

Some approach midlife as a critical juncture;
however, the Chinese spell "crisis" by combining
the symbol for "danger" with the symbol
for "opportunity"!

GAP.

INFANCY

ADOLESCENCE

OLD AGE

The subject of midlife has been largely neglected
until recently; now they're even making movies
about it.

LONGEVITY.

In the Olden Days, there wasn't any time for a
midlife. You last longer now.

BOXED.

Census figures predict that 22% of U.S. men will find themselves in the midlife male box by 1985.

RECOGNITION.

Midlife isn't exactly chronological or logical. It occurs somewhere between 30 and 40. Unless it happens earlier . . . or later.

"You know you're getting old when the candles cost more than the cake." —BOB HOPE

"Middle age is when your clothes no longer fit, and it's you who need the alteration." —EARL WILSON

"The hormone production level is dropping, the head is balding, the sexual vigor is diminishing, the stress is unending, the children are leaving, the parents are dying, the job horizons are narrowing, the friends are having their first heart attacks: the past floats by in a fog of hopes not realized, opportunities not grasped, women not bedded, potential not fulfilled, and the future is a confrontation with one's own mortality." —MARTHA LEAR

"Middle Age is when you've met so many people that every new person you meet reminds you of someone else." —OGDEN NASH

"What I would really like to do is sit under a tree with a glass of wine in my hand and watch the dancers." —ADLAI STEVENSON

"Middle age is the time when a man is always thinking that in a week or two he will feel just as good as ever." —DON MARQUIS

CHANGE.

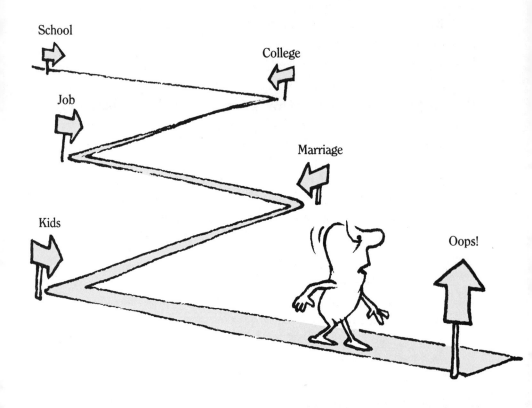

The most reliable characteristic of midlife is change.

UNCERTAINTY.

Many changes are unexpected. Some are unnerving.

DOUBT.

Your self-image is also changing, if you stop to think
about it.   And you do.

STUCK.

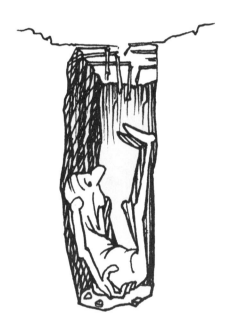

Midlife can be the pits; going nowhere, in your work,
your interests, your marriage, and in other
sticky areas.

RUNDOWN.

A certain downhill nature of things is still another
midlife tip-off.

OVERRUN.

And a daily buildup of pressure is a certain signal.

LIFE &
DEATH.

"No one believes in his own death . . . in the
unconscious everyone is convinced of his
own immortality."

—Sigmund Freud

"Old age is like a plane flying through a storm. Once you're aboard, there's nothing you can do." —GOLDA MEIR

"The most important learnings are internal, intrinsic; one learns more from the death of a parent than from all the academic subjects one studies." —ABRAHAM MASLOW

"Age doesn't matter, unless you're cheese."
—BILLIE BURKE

"When you sit with a nice girl for two hours you think it's only a minute. But when you sit on a hot stove for a minute, you think it's two hours. That's relativity."
—ALBERT EINSTEIN

"Old age is not so bad, when you consider the alternative."
—MAURICE CHEVALIER

"I've come to look upon death the same way I look upon root-canal work. Everyone else seems to get through it all right, so it couldn't be too difficult for me." —JOSEPH HELLER

"Death is not the greatest loss in life. The greatest loss is what dies inside us while we live." —NORMAN COUSINS

"The awareness that time is finite is a particularly conspicuous feature of middle age. Life is restructured in terms of the time-left-to-live rather than time-since-birth."
—BERNICE L. NEUGARTEN, PH.D.

TIME.

Time, once so friendly and helpful in poaching eggs, is not to be trusted. It's actually running out on you.

UNBELIEVABLE.

Of all your undertakings, this one is the only
sure thing.

NEXT!

When a parent dies, the loss includes any remaining
innocence about your own mortality.

ENODY.

The way we accumulate possessions, you'd think the
Final Journey had a baggage allowance.

FINITO.

Running out of time is what makes basketball,
football, and game shows interesting. This is seldom
true in end-of-the-line situations.

WHOA!

Time accelerates at the midlife station. Years flicker
by like telephone poles. Give yourself a brake. Find
time for the wildflowers.

GLUT.

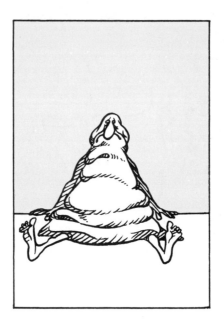

"Middle age is when your age starts to show around your middle."

—BOB HOPE

"Middle age is when anything new in the way you feel is most likely a symptom." —LAURENCE PETER

"Learn to be selfish about your body. One ultimate value of life will always be health. A vibrantly healthy man is an attractive man. Without it joylessness and meaninglessness become an increasingly present reality." —HERB GOLDBERG, PH.D.

"Health is a task. Success in this personal task is in large part the result of self-awareness, self-discipline and inner resources." —IVAN ILLICH

"Wanting to live longer and be healthy is a part of why I exercise, but mainly it's a mental thing. Exercise adds life to my years—in addition to years to my life." —CHARLES KUNTZLEMAN, PH.D.

"Get real exercise. Keep your weight down. Keep moving and keep thinking. Too many people die from Disuse of their Bodies." —DR. PAUL DUDLEY WHITE

"You know you've reached middle age when your weight lifting consists of standing up." —BOB HOPE

"All the things I really like to do are either immoral, illegal, or fattening." —ALEXANDER WOOLLCOTT

LOSS.

In the middle years—while losing fitness, idealism,
and hair—you gain weight.   A miserable swap.

LETHARGY.

You've also traded rock 'n' roll for slump and sag.

INTAKE.

You are what you eat . . . more or less.

INCONSISTENCY.

Occasional exercise, and occasional diets, can be
expected to produce occasional longevity.

BOOZE.

Don't stay on the bottle; you gave it up at age two,
so try again.

BOOB.

Rumor has it that there's more to life than
beer and TV.

SELF.

The trouble with the American work ethic is that it encourages a man to become what he does. This seems to work out for doctors and anchormen, but could be disastrous for Hula-Hoop salesmen.

"Who in the world am I? Ah, that's the great puzzle."
—LEWIS CARROLL

"Not in the clamor of the crowded streets
Not in the shouts and plaudits of the throng
But in ourselves, are triumphs and defeat."
—HENRY WADSWORTH LONGFELLOW

"If you become addicted to work and then become obsolete, what the hell have you got left?"
—HARRISON M. TRICE, PH.D.

"It is not a matter of how many rewards one has obtained; it is a matter of the goodness of fit between the life structure and the self. A man may do extremely well in achieving his goals and yet find his success hollow or bittersweet."
—DANIEL LEVINSON, PH.D.

"The real voyage of discovery consists not in seeking new landscapes, but in having new eyes."
—MARCEL PROUST

"People should not consider so much what they are to do, as what they are."
—MASTER ECKHART

"Self-love, my liege, is not so vile a sin as self-neglecting."
—SHAKESPEARE

"To love oneself is the beginning of a lifelong romance."
—OSCAR WILDE

ACHIEVEMENT.

So here you are at midlife, naked with your
merit badges.

AWARDS.

No matter what rewards you've gained, there's always
something better.   Maybe.

SURPRISE.

What you have is not who you are.

LOST.

When career aims cause you to miss life's satisfactions, it's no way to run an airline.

REVEAL.

In self-examination, of course, there's always the
danger of discovering the truth.

APPEAL.

Yet, in discovering your diversity, you'll find there's a lot to like.

EXAMINE.

Review those old behavior patterns that were set in
your youth.

RELY.

Once you understand yourself, stay in touch.

FAMILY.

"Age doesn't protect you from love. But love, to
some extent, protects you from age."
—JEANNE MOREAU

"Oh, what a tough web do parents weave when they think their children are naive." —OGDEN NASH

"I am protected as if by a charm by the presence within me of my family and comrades." —PETER MARIN

"In general those parents have the most reverence who deserve it; for he that lives well cannot be despised." —SAMUEL JOHNSON

"Children have more need of models than of critics." —JOUBERT

"I have found the best way to give advice to your children is to find out what they want and then advise them to do it." —HARRY S. TRUMAN

"Wife and children are a kind of discipline of humanity." —FRANCIS BACON

"It is not enough for parents to understand children. They must grant children the privilege of understanding them." —MILTON R. SAPERSTEIN

HERO.

These days, your heroic role with the balancing pole
seems largely unappreciated.

SQUARE.

Once you had so much in common, but nobody
wants to color Easter eggs anymore.

VIEW.

There's a distinct possibility that you may have
learned something from your kids.

REVIEW.

However, support of their extracurricular activities is
due for review about now.

BURDENED.

After all these years, there should be carrying
charges (for carrying charges).

BONDAGE.

While adjusting all these midlife burdens, don't
forget to take out the garbage.

PARENTS.

Raising you wasn't enough; now they may want to
raise a little hell.

CHILDHOOD.

It's better the second time around.

NICHE.

Instead of groceries, she's now carrying six hours of French, ten units of economics, and a karate class.

DITCH.

She's finding her identity, and you're wondering
where yours went.

SWITCH.

The "head of the house" now refers to the bathroom.

ENRICH.

Now that "obey" is officially out of the vow, you can
live nicely with "love" and "honor."

SEX.

"... with most men, sexual problems are
in the mind."

—Dr. H. Lear

"The most pernicious of all sexual fictions is the nearly universally accepted belief that sexual effectiveness inevitably disappears as the human being ages. It simply isn't true."
—WILLIAM H. MASTERS &
VIRGINIA E. JOHNSON

"After thirty-five a penis becomes more difficult to train and impossible to command. Like a car's motorized antenna it requires a live battery, the ignition key turned, and someone to push the right button. If all the things aren't working, it won't function. You can pull on it all you want."
—ARNOLD J. MANDELL, M.D.

"The difference between sex and death is with death you can do it alone and nobody's going to make fun of you."
—WOODY ALLEN

"I think anything is all right provided it is done in private and doesn't frighten the horses."   —BRENDAN BEHAN

"When I was young I used to have success with women because I was young. Now I have success with women because I am old. Middle age was the hard part."
—ARTHUR RUBINSTEIN

"The only unnatural sex act is that which you cannot perform."   —ALFRED KINSEY

EXTINGUISHED.

Any day now, your distinguished cache of erotica will lose its charm.

REFRESHED.

The mutual attraction of older men and younger women is nature's way of testing your character or your endurance.

INEQUALITY.

She's been liberated, but a constitutional Equal
Rights Amendment won't change unequal aging.

PERFORMANCE.

Jogging, juggling, and jiggling may be amusing, but
the best act in a love story isn't tough . . . it's tender.

REVOLTING.

Usually reliable soldiers have been known to go
AWOL quite unexpectedly. It's best to forgive
and forget.

DELIGHTFUL.

Loving, sharing, joyful sex unfolds in midlife—with less frequency but with more satisfaction—and continues into old age.

PALS.

"A man cannot be said to succeed in this life who
does not satisfy one friend."

—THOREAU

"Friendship is nothing else than an accord in all things, human and divine, conjoined with much good will and affection." —CICERO

"Never contract a friendship with a man that is not better than thyself." —CONFUCIUS

"The love of man to woman is a thing common and of course, and at first partakes more of instinct and passion than of choice; but true friendship between man and man is infinite and immortal." —PLATO

"It is great to have friends when one is young, but indeed it is still more so when you are getting old. When we are young, friends are, like everything else, a matter of course. In the old days we know what it means to have them.
—EDVARD GRIEG

"A true friend unbosoms freely, advises justly, assists readily, adventures boldly, takes all patiently, defends courageously, and continues a friend unchangeably." —WILLIAM PENN

"Friendship is the hardest thing in the world to explain. It's not something you learn in school. But if you haven't learned the meaning of friendship, you really haven't learned anything." —MUHAMMAD ALI

"In life you throw a ball. You hope it will reach a wall and bounce back so you can throw it again. You hope your friends will provide that wall." —PABLO PICASSO

ALONE.

Your midlife spacewalk is essentially a solo mission.

RESPONSIBLE.

Despite other connections, you're alone
and responsible.

CLOSENESS.

Some old ties are just as out-of-date as your other old ties.

OPENNESS.

Friendship is like a book; it's got to be open and
understood to be enjoyed.

TOGETHERNESS.

The toughest bind is separating the friends from
the freight.

BONDS.

But cherish your pals. A good man nowadays is hard
to find.

CHANGES &
CHOICES.

You're between what you were and what you may
become. A choice position.

"At twenty years of age the will reigns; at thirty the wit; at forty the judgment." —BENJAMIN FRANKLIN

"As a man advances in life he gets what is better than admiration—judgment to estimate things at their own value." —SAMUEL JOHNSON

"The shortest and surest way to live with honor in the world is to be in reality what we appear to be." —SOCRATES

"If you treat man as he appears to be, you make him worse than he is. But if you treat man as if he already was what he potentially could be, you make him what he should be." —GOETHE

"When choosing between two evils, I always like to take the one I've never tried before." —MAE WEST

"I have learned to seek my happiness by limiting my desires, rather than in attempting to satisfy them." —JOHN STUART MILL

"The very frequent neurotic disturbances of adult years all have one thing in common. They want to carry the psychology of the youthful phase over the threshold of the so-called years of discretion." —C. G. JUNG

"There is more to life than increasing its speed." —MAHATMA GANDHI

GO.

Although you may drift placidly into midlife,
there are big changes ahead.

STOP.

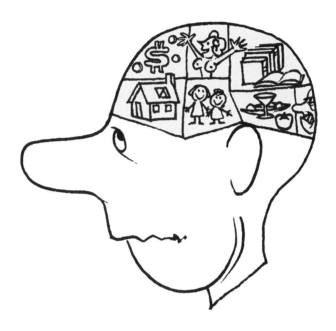

Your mental blocks of past patterns resist change.

GROWTH.

Change is inevitable—and synonymous with life.

DECISIONS.

Some changes involve giving up power
and responsibility.

CHANCE.

Risking change isn't easy; you might fail.

OPTIMISM.

Risking failure is imperative to growth.

PISSIMISM.

Failure is a necessary part of learning.

FANTASY.

Midlife's a good place to try on your dreams for size.

MYTHS.

"We are handicapped by policies based on old myths
rather than current realities."
—JAMES W. FULBRIGHT

"Retirement at sixty-five is ridiculous. When I was sixty-five I still had pimples." —GEORGE BURNS

"Experience is not what happens to a man. It is what a man does with what happens to him." —ALDOUS HUXLEY

"He that has seen both sides of fifty has lived to little purpose if he has not other views of the world than he had when he was much younger." —WILLIAM COWPER

"The only things worth learning are the things you learn after you know it all." —HARRY TRUMAN

"It sometimes takes a heart attack to make one realize how much we've been sustaining ourselves with fantasies." —DR. ROY MENNINGER

"You don't have to suffer continual chaos in order to grow." —JOHN C. LILLY

"Life does not need to be changed. Only our attitudes do." —SRI SWAMI RAMA

"The game is not about becoming somebody, it's about becoming nobody." —BABA RAM DASS

CONTINUED.

Myths persist because they lend themselves more
often to embroidery than to examination.

DISCONTINUED.

It's about time you found out what you've
been mything.

MYTHCONSTRUED.

Are diminishing opportunities a myth . . .
or a reality?

MYTHTAKEN.

Is tunnel vision somewhat limiting your view?

MYTHUNDERSTOOD.

Is the approval of others as important as your
own self-esteem?

MYTHJUDGMENT.

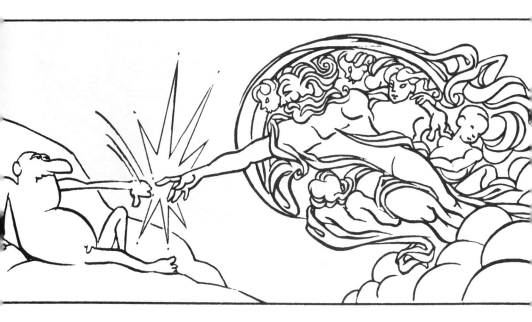

Do you still think that the Lord is going to make an
exception in your case?

MYTHLED.

Have you really overcome your Macho Myth?

MYTHCONCEPTION.

How about the rumored sexual dysfunction
at midlife?

MYTHPLACED.

If you can get past the myths and fables, you're ready

to live in the best place: the present.

GOALS.

"The goal of life is living in agreement with nature."
—EPICURUS

"In three words I can sum up everything I've learned about life. It goes on."　　　　　　　　—ROBERT FROST

"My son, if you have the means, treat yourself well. For there is no pleasure in the grave, and there is no postponement of death."　　　—RABBI BEN SIRA, SECOND CENTURY B.C.

"I am at that point of my life when it behooves each one to lower sail, and haul in sheet."　　　　　　　—DANTE

"Men have never fully used the powers they possess to advance the good in life, because they have waited upon some power external to themselves and to nature to do the work they are responsible for doing."　　　—JOHN DEWEY

"It takes one a long time to become young."
　　　　　　　　　—PABLO PICASSO

"He who loves money will never have enough of it, and he who loves wealth will never attain it."
　　　　　　　　—ECCLESIASTES 5:10

"When one turns his attention inward he discovers a world of 'inner space' which is as vast and as 'real' as the external, physical world."　　　—WILLIS HARMON

MEDITATE.

Another midlife exercise is contemplating your
goals, external and internal.

CONCENTRATE.

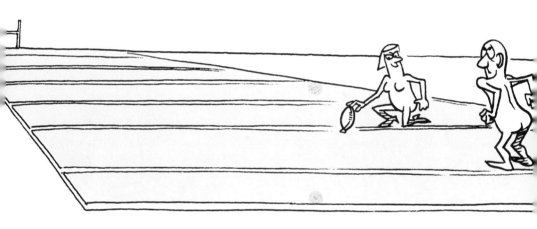

Are you working toward altogether reasonable and
achievable objectives?

EXTRICATE.

Escape from what others think you should do is an
OK external goal.

LIBERATE.

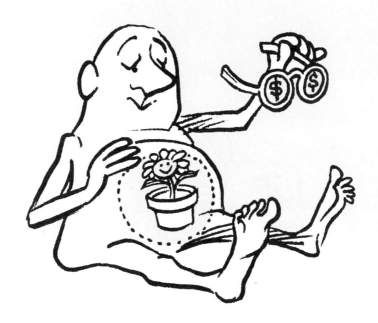

Do you *have* internal goals . . . like discovering your
true feelings?

RETALIATE.

Release of suppressed emotions is a worthwhile goal.

DELEGATE.

There's no need to act your age, to act young,
or to act.

SEPARATE.

Happiness is not a goal; it's a by-product of life.

CELEBRATE.

With myths behind you and internal/external goals
ahead, you can be Mr. Wonderful today!

ACTION.

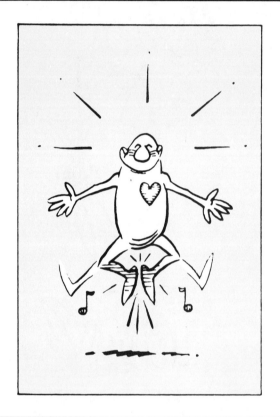

"God respects me when I work, but He loves me when I sing."

—TAGORE

"The most beautiful experience we can have is the mysterious. It is the fundamental emotion which stands at the cradle of true art and true science. Whoever does not know it and can no longer wonder, no longer marvel, is as good as dead, and his eyes are dimmed." —ALBERT EINSTEIN

"Every man must render an account before God of all the good things he beheld in life and did not enjoy."
—THE TALMUD

"Perhaps one can shed at this stage of life, as one sheds in beach-living, one's pride, one's false ambitions, one's mask, one's armor. Was that armor not put on to protect one from the competitive world? If one ceases to compete does one need it? Perhaps one can, at last, in middle age, be completely one-self? What a liberation that would be!"
—ANNE MORROW LINDBERGH

"No problem is so big and complicated that it can't be run away from." —CHARLIE BROWN

"Much of the lethargy in a decaying social system is traceable to the large number of individuals who no longer believe in what they are doing. Those who can find something to believe in and work for are granted a blessed release from emptiness." —JOHN GARDNER

"I will take life by the throat. It shall not wholly overcome me." —LUDWIG VAN BEETHOVEN

"We know what we are, but know not what we may be."
—WILLIAM SHAKESPEARE

REMOVE.

A good start is getting rid of unfinished business.

BOOM.

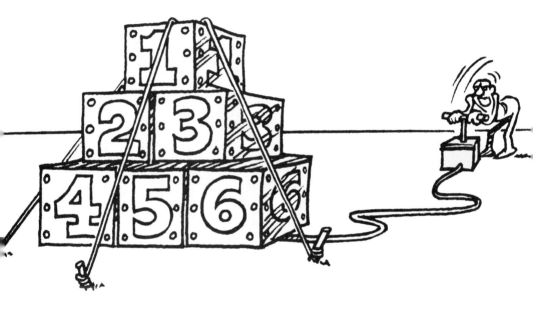

Your next move is to rearrange your priorities.

TOOLS.

Rediscover your stored skills.

JEWELS.

Reawaken dormant interests.

SWING.

Revive your sense of play.

SWAY.

Find your best balance of work and play.

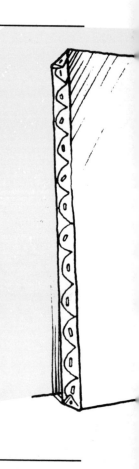

START.

Finally explore your creative potential.
(Start anywhere!)

BEGINNING.

"But still I dream that somewhere there must be
The spirit of a child that waits for me."
—BAYARD TAYLOR

"If you would not age, you must make everything you do touched with play, play of the body, of thought, of emotions. If you do, you will belong to that special class of people who find joy and happiness in every act, in every moment."
—GEORGE SHEEHAN, M.D.

"Grow old along with me! The best is yet to be."
—ROBERT BROWNING

"For age is opportunity no less than youth itself, though in another dress, and as the evening twilight fades away the sky is filled with stars, invisible by day."
—HENRY WADSWORTH LONGFELLOW

"Each day I must begin again as a rediscovery of the world of which I have the joy to be a part."   —PABLO CASALS

"Human beings can alter their lives by altering their attitudes of mind."   —WILLIAM JAMES

"To be what we are, and to become what we are capable of becoming is the only end of life."   —WILLIAM JAMES

"The individual has within himself vast resources for self-understanding, for altering his self-concept, his attitudes and his self-directed behavior."   —CARL ROGERS

QUESTION.

We've raised some midlife questions, and suggested some answers:

ANSWER.

It's not the years you've lived that count . . . it's the
ones you've got left.

FLY.

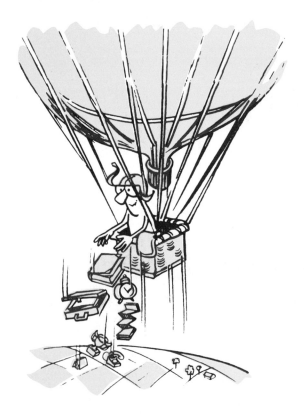

Toss out the accumulations, patterns, and baggage
of the past.

TRY.

Take it from the top . . . this time with feeling!

REWIND.

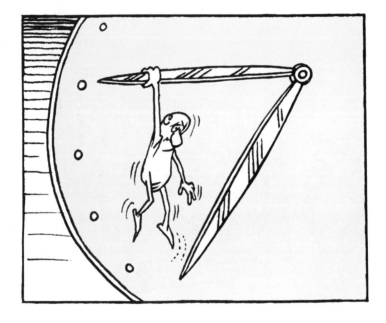

Time has a different meaning now. Although you probably flunked adolescence and missed the sexual revolution altogether, here's a second chance.

MIDLIFE.

Share it with someone you love.

JACK ROBERTS, cartoonist/writer, entered advertising long before midlife. With partner Ralph Carson, he built Carson/Roberts into the West's largest and most successful independent advertising agency, which merged, in 1971, with Ogilvy & Mather. Roberts's first book was a cartoon guide for weekend whackers, *So You're Going to Take Tennis Seriously?*

DICK GUNTHER, behaviorist/writer, took a midlife turn away from a prosperous real estate business into research and participation in the Humanistic/Transformational field. His focus now is not only male midlife, but also a mix of family and friends, marathons and tennis, civic and religious commitments, continuing education, and personal growth.

STAN GORTIKOV, editor/writer, spends his midlife days as president of the Recording Industry Association of America, the trade association of recording companies. For eleven prior years he nested at Capitol Records, where he was president. Still earlier, he worked in the garment industry and in advertising/journalism. A combination of career changes and marital experiences has molded him into a walking model of midlife dynamics.